MODERN DEMOCRACY

BY

CARL L. BECKER

JOHN WENDELL ANDERSON PROFESSOR OF HISTORY
IN CORNELL UNIVERSITY

NEW HAVEN
YALE UNIVERSITY PRESS
LONDON · HUMPHREY MILFORD · OXFORD UNIVERSITY PRESS
1941

Thought makes the whole dignity of man;
therefore endeavor to think well, that is the
only morality.

PASCAL

PREFACE

THIS small volume contains three lectures delivered at the University of Virginia, on the Page-Barbour Foundation, November 12–14, 1940. Except for a few verbal changes they are printed as given. To plagiarize one's own writings is not a commendable practice; but in a few instances I have made use of passages already in print elsewhere. The only really deplorable instance, the only passage, that is to say, that runs to more than a few sentences, is on pages 19–23—five paragraphs taken from "Afterthoughts on Constitutions," first published in the Yale Review, XXVII, 455.

I gladly take this opportunity to express to President Newcomb and members of the faculty my appreciation of all that was done, with so much friendly and thoughtful consideration for me personally, to make my short visit to the University an occasion to be always remembered.

CARL BECKER

Ithaca, New York,
  November, 1940.

CONTENTS

PREFACE   vii

I. THE IDEAL   1

II. THE REALITY   31

III. THE DILEMMA   65

I

THE IDEAL

Natural law is the regular and constant order of facts by which God rules the universe; the order which his wisdom presents to the sense and reason of men, to serve them as an equal and common rule of conduct, and to guide them, without distinction of race or sect, toward perfection and happiness.   VOLNEY

I OFTEN find it difficult, when invited to speak before a university audience, to hit upon a proper subject. But the invitation to deliver the Page-Barbour lectures at the University of Virginia relieved me of that difficulty: the invitation itself, automatically so to speak, conveniently laid the proper subject in my lap. For the University of Virginia is inseparably associated with the name of its famous founder; and no subject, it seemed to me, could be more appropriate for a historian on this occasion than one which had some connection with the ideas or the activities of Thomas Jefferson.

Even so, you will rightly think, I had a sufficiently wide choice. Jefferson entertained so many ideas, was engaged in so many activities! There was, indeed, scarcely anything of human interest that was alien to his curious and far-ranging intelligence. Nevertheless, his name is always associated with a certain general idea, a certain ideal. In devising his own epitaph, Jefferson himself selected, out of all his notable achievements, only three for which he wished to be especially remembered. *Here was buried Thomas Jefferson, author of the Declaration of American Independence, of the Statute of Virginia for Religious Freedom, and Father of the University of Virginia.* These were the things for which he wished to be remembered. Taken together and in their implications, they are the things for which he has been remembered: that is to say, they conveniently symbolize that way of looking at man and the life of man, that social philosophy, which we always think of when we think of him. The word which best denotes this social philosophy is democracy. I feel sure, therefore, that here, in this famous center of learning, you will not think it inappropriate for me to say something, something relevant if that be at all possible, about democracy—a subject so close to Jefferson's heart and so insistently present in all our minds today.

Democracy, like liberty or science or progress, is a word with which we are all so familiar that we rarely take the trouble to ask what we mean by it. It is a term, as the devotees of semantics say, which has no "referent"—there is no precise or palpable thing or object which we all think of when the word is pronounced. On the contrary, it is a word which connotes different things to different people, a kind of conceptual Gladstone bag which, with a little manipulation, can be made to accommodate almost any collection of social facts we may wish to carry about in it. In

4

it we can as easily pack a dictatorship as any other form of government. We have only to stretch the concept to include any form of government supported by a majority of the people, for whatever reasons and by whatever means of expressing assent, and before we know it the empire of Napoleon, the Soviet regime of Stalin, and the Fascist systems of Mussolini and Hitler are all safely *included* in the bag. But if this is what we mean by democracy, then virtually all forms of government are democratic, since virtually all governments, except in times of revolution, rest upon the explicit or implicit consent of the people. In order to discuss democracy intelligently it will be necessary, therefore, to define it, to attach to the word a sufficiently precise meaning to avoid the confusion which is not infrequently the chief result of such discussions.

All human institutions, we are told, have their ideal forms laid away in heaven, and we do not need to be told that the actual institutions conform but indifferently to these ideal counterparts. It would be possible then to define democracy either in terms of the ideal or in terms of the real form—to define it as government of the people, by the people, for the people; or to define it as government of the people, by the politicians, for whatever pressure groups can get their interests taken care of. But as a historian I am naturally disposed to be satisfied with the meaning which, in the history of politics, men have commonly attributed to the word—a meaning, needless to say, which derives partly from the experience and partly from the aspirations of mankind. So regarded, the term democracy refers primarily to a form of government, and it has always meant government by the many as opposed to government by the one—government by the people as opposed to government by a tyrant, a dictator, or an absolute monarch. This is the most general meaning of the word as men have commonly understood it.

In this antithesis there are, however, certain implications, always tacitly understood, which give a more precise meaning to the term. Peisistratus, for example, was supported by a majority of the people, but his government was never regarded as a democracy for all that. Caesar's power derived from a popular mandate, conveyed through established republican forms, but that did not make his government any the less a dictatorship. Napoleon called his government a democratic empire, but no one, least of all Napoleon himself, doubted that he had destroyed the last vestiges of the democratic republic. Since the Greeks first used the term, the essential test of democratic government has always been this: the source of political authority must be and remain in the people and not in the ruler. A democratic government has always meant one in which the citizens, or a sufficient number of them to represent more or less effectively the common will, freely act from time to time, and according to established forms, to appoint or recall the magistrates and to enact or revoke the laws by which the community is governed. This I take to be the meaning which history has impressed upon the term democracy as a form of government. It is, therefore, the meaning which I attach to it in these lectures.

The most obvious political fact of our time is that democracy as thus defined has suffered an astounding decline in prestige. Fifty years ago it was not impossible to regard democratic government, and the liberties that went with it, as a permanent conquest of the human spirit. In 1886 Andrew Carnegie published a book entitled *Triumphant Democracy*. Written without fear and without research, the book was not an achievement of the highest intellectual distinction perhaps; but the title at least expressed well enough the prevailing conviction—the conviction that democracy had fought the good fight, had won the decisive battles, and would inevitably, through its inherent merits, presently banish from the world the most flagrant political and social evils which from time immemorial had afflicted mankind. This conviction could no doubt be most easily entertained in the United States, where even the tradition of other forms of government was too remote and alien to color our native optimism. But even in Europe the downright skeptics, such as Lecky, were thought to be perverse, and so hardheaded a historian as J. B. Bury could proclaim with confidence that the long struggle for freedom of thought had finally been won.

I do not need to tell you that within a brief twenty years the prevailing optimism of that time has been quite dispelled. One European country after another has, willingly enough it seems, abandoned whatever democratic institutions it formerly enjoyed for some form of dictatorship. The spokesmen of Fascism and Communism announce with confidence that democracy, a sentimental aberration which the world has outgrown, is done for; and even the friends of democracy support it with declining conviction. They tell us that democracy, so far from being triumphant, is "at the cross roads" or "in retreat," and that its future is by no means assured. What are we to

8

think of this sudden reversal in fortune and prestige? How explain it? What to do about it?

II

One of the presuppositions of modern thought is that institutions, in order to be understood, must be seen in relation to the conditions of time and place in which they appear. It is a little difficult for us to look at democracy in this way. We are so immersed in its present fortunes that we commonly see it only as a "close-up," filling the screen to the exclusion of other things to which it is in fact related. In order to form an objective judgment of its nature and significance, we must therefore first of all get it in proper perspective. Let us then, in imagination, remove from the immediate present scene to some cool high place where we can survey at a glance five or six thousand years of history, and note the part which democracy has played in human civilization. The view, if we have been accustomed to take democratic institutions for granted, is a bit bleak and disheartening. For we see at once that in all this long time, over the habitable globe, the great majority of the human race has neither known

9

nor apparently much cared for our favorite institutions.

Civilization was already old when democracy made its first notable appearance among the small city states of ancient Greece, where it flourished brilliantly for a brief century or two and then disappeared. At about the same time something that might be called democracy appeared in Rome and other Italian cities, but even in Rome it did not survive the conquest of the world by the Roman Republic, except as a form of local administration in the cities of the empire. In the twelfth and thirteenth centuries certain favorably placed medieval cities enjoyed a measure of self-government, but in most instances it was soon replaced by the dictatorship of military conquerors, the oligarchic control of a few families, or the encroaching power of autocratic kings. The oldest democracy of modern times is the Swiss Confederation, the next oldest is the Dutch Republic. Parliamentary government in England does not antedate the late seventeenth century, the great American experiment is scarcely older. Not until the nineteenth century did democratic government make its way in any considerable part of the world—in the great states of continental Europe, in South America, in Canada and Australia, in South Africa and Japan.

THE IDEAL

From this brief survey it is obvious that, taking the experience of mankind as a test, democracy has as yet had but a limited and temporary success. There must be a reason for this significant fact. The reason is that democratic government is a species of social luxury, at best a delicate and precarious adventure which depends for success upon the validity of certain assumptions about the capacities and virtues of men, and upon the presence of certain material and intellectual conditions favorable to the exercise of these capacities and virtues. Let us take the material conditions first.

It is a striking fact that until recently democracy never flourished except in very small states —for the most part in cities. It is true that in both the Persian and the Roman empires a measure of self-government was accorded to local communities, but only in respect to purely local affairs; in no large state as a whole was democratic government found to be practicable. One essential reason is that until recently the means of communication were too slow and uncertain to create the necessary solidarity of interest and similarity of information over large areas. The principle of representation was well enough known to the Greeks, but in practice it proved impracticable except in limited areas and for

11

special occasions. As late as the eighteenth century it was still the common opinion that the republican form of government, although the best ideally, was unsuited to large countries, even to a country no larger than France. This was the view of Montesquieu, and even of Rousseau. The view persisted into the nineteenth century, and English conservatives, who were opposed to the extension of the suffrage in England, consoled themselves with the notion that the American Civil War would confirm it—would demonstrate that government by and for the people would perish, if not from off the earth at least from large countries. If their hopes were confounded the reason is that the means of communication, figuratively speaking, were making large countries small. It is not altogether fanciful to suppose that, but for the railroad and the telegraph, the United States would today be divided into many small republics maneuvering for advantage and employing war and diplomacy for maintaining an unstable balance of power.

If one of the conditions essential to the success of democratic government is mobility, ease of communication, another is a certain measure of economic security. Democracy does not flourish in communities on the verge of destitution. In ancient and medieval times democratic government appeared for the most part in cities, the centers of prosperity. Farmers in the early Roman Republic and in the Swiss Cantons were not wealthy to be sure, but equality of possessions and of opportunity gave them a certain economic security. In medieval cities political privilege was confined to the prosperous merchants and crafts- men, and in Athens and the later Roman Repub- lic democratic government was found to be work- able only on condition that the poor citizens were subsidized by the government or paid for attend- ing the assemblies and the law courts.

In modern times democratic institutions have, generally speaking, been most successful in new countries, such as the United States, Canada, and Australia, where the conditions of life have been easy for the people; and in European countries more or less in proportion to their industrial pros- perity. In European countries, indeed, there has been a close correlation between the development of the industrial revolution and the emergence of democratic institutions. Holland and England, the first countries to experience the industrial revolution, were the first also (apart from Switzer- land, where certain peculiar conditions obtained) to adopt democratic institutions; and as the in- dustrial revolution spread to France, Belgium, Germany, and Italy, these countries in turn adopted at least a measure of democratic government. Democracy is in some sense an economic luxury, and it may be said that in modern times it has been a function of the development of new and potentially rich countries, or of the industrial revolution which suddenly dowered Europe with unaccustomed wealth. Now that prosperity is disappearing round every next corner, democracy works less well than it did.

So much for the material conditions essential for the success of democratic government. Supposing these conditions to exist, democratic government implies in addition the presence of certain capacities and virtues in its citizens. These capacities and virtues are bound up with the assumptions on which democracy rests, and are available only in so far as the assumptions are valid. The primary assumption of democratic government is that its citizens are capable of managing their own affairs. But life in any community involves a conflict of individual and class interests, and a corresponding divergence of opinion as to the measures to be adopted for the common good. The divergent opinions must be somehow reconciled, the conflict of interests somehow compromised. It must then be an assumption of democratic government that its citizens are rational creatures, sufficiently so at least

14

to understand the interests in conflict; and it must be an assumption that they are men of good will, sufficiently so toward each other at least to make those concessions of individual and class interest required for effecting workable compromises. The citizens of a democracy should be, as Pericles said the citizens of Athens were, if not all originators at least all sound judges of good policy.

These are what may be called the minimum assumptions and the necessary conditions of democratic government anywhere and at any time. They may be noted to best advantage, not in any state, but in small groups within the state—in clubs and similar private associations of congenial and like-minded people united for a specific purpose. In such associations the membership is limited and select. The members are, or may easily become, all acquainted with each other. Everyone knows, or may easily find out, what is being done and who is doing it. There will of course be differences of opinion, and there may be disintegrating squabbles and intrigues. But on the whole, ends and means being specific and well understood, the problems of government are few and superficial; there is plenty of time for discussion; and since intelligence and good will can generally be taken for granted there is the dis-

position to make reasonable concessions and compromises. The analogy must be taken for what
it is worth. States may not be the mystical blind
Molochs of German philosophy, but any state is
far more complex and intangible than a private
association, and there is little resemblance between such associations and the democracies of
modern times. Other things equal, the resemblance is closest in very small states, and it is in
connection with the small city states of ancient
Greece that the resemblance can best be noted.

The Greek states were limited in size, not as is
often thought solely or even chiefly by the physi-
ography of the country, but by some instinctive
feeling of the Greek mind that a state is necessarily a natural association of people bound together by ties of kinship and a common tradition
of rights and obligations. There must then, as
Aristotle said, be a limit.

For if the citizens of a state are to judge and distribute offices according to merit, they must know
each other's characters; where they do not possess
this knowledge, both the elections to offices and the
decisions in the law courts will go wrong. Where the
population is very large they are manifestly settled
by haphazard, which clearly ought not to be. Besides, in overpopulous states foreigners and metics

will readily acquire citizenship, for who will find
them out?

It obviously did not occur to Aristotle that metics
and foreigners should be free to acquire citizenship. It did not occur to him, or to any Greek of
his time, or to the merchants of the self-governing
medieval city, that a state should be composed of
all the people inhabiting a given territory. A state
was rather an incorporated body of people within,
but distinct from, the population of the community.

Ancient and medieval democracies had thus
something of the character of a private association. They were, so to speak, purely pragmatic
phenomena, arising under very special conditions,
and regarded as the most convenient way of
managing the affairs of people bound together by
community of interest and for the achievement of
specific ends. There is no suggestion in Aristotle
that democracy (polity) is intrinsically a superior
form of government, no suggestion that it derives from a special ideology of its own. If it rests
upon any superiority other than convenience, it is
the superiority which it shares with any Greek
state, that is to say, the superiority of Greek over
barbarian civilization. In Aristotle's philosophy it

is indeed difficult to find any clear-cut distinction between the democratic form of government and the state itself; the state, if it be worthy of the name, is always, whatever the form of government, "the government of freemen and equals," and in any state it is always necessary that "the freemen who compose the bulk of the people should have absolute power in some things." In Aristotle's philosophy the distinction between good and bad in politics is not between good and bad types of government, but between the good and the bad form of each type. Any type of government—monarchy, aristocracy, polity—is good provided the rulers aim at the good of all rather than at the good of the class to which they belong. From Aristotle's point of view neither democracy nor dictatorship is good or bad in itself, but only in the measure that it achieves, or fails to achieve, the aim of every good state, which is that "the inhabitants of it should be happy." It did not occur to Aristotle that democracy (polity), being in some special sense in harmony with the nature of man, was everywhere applicable, and therefore destined by fate or the gods to carry throughout the world a superior form of civilization.

It is in this respect chiefly that modern democracy differs from earlier forms. It rests upon something more than the minimum assumptions. It is reinforced by a full-blown ideology which, by endowing the individual with natural and imprescriptible rights, sets the democratic form of government off from all others as the one which alone can achieve the good life. What then are the essential tenets of the modern democratic faith?

III

THE liberal democratic faith, as expressed in the works of eighteenth and early nineteenth-century writers, is one of the formulations of the modern doctrine of progress. It will be well, therefore, to note briefly the historical antecedents of that doctrine.

In the long history of man on earth there comes a time when he remembers something of what has been, anticipates something that will be, knows the country he has traversed, wonders what lies beyond—the moment when he becomes aware of himself as a lonely, differentiated item in the world. Sooner or later there emerges for him the most devastating of all facts, namely, that in an indifferent universe which alone endures, he alone aspires, endeavors to attain, and attains only to be defeated in the end. From that

19

moment his immediate experience ceases to be adequate, and he endeavors to project himself beyond it by creating ideal worlds of semblance, Utopias of other time or place in which all has been, may be, or will be well.

In ancient times Utopia was most easily projected into the unknown past, pushed back to the beginning of things—to the time of P'an Ku and the celestial emperors, to the Garden of Eden, or the reign of King Chronos when men lived like gods free from toil and grief. From this happy state of first created things there had obviously been a decline and fall, occasioned by disobedience and human frailty, and decreed as punishment by fate or the angry gods. The mind of man was therefore afflicted with pessimism, a sense of guilt for having betrayed the divine purpose, a feeling of inadequacy for bringing the world back to its original state of innocence and purity. To men who felt insecure in a changing world, and helpless in a world always changing for the worse, the future had little to offer. It could be regarded for the most part only with resignation, mitigated by individual penance or welldoing, or the hope of some miraculous intervention by the gods, or the return of the god-like kings, to set things right again, yet with little hope that from this setting right there would not be another falling away.

This pervasive pessimism was gradually dispelled in the Western world, partly by the Christian religion, chiefly by the secular intellectual revolution occurring roughly between the fifteenth and the eighteenth centuries. The Christian religion gave assurance that the lost golden age of the past would be restored for the virtuous in the future, and by proclaiming the supreme worth of the individual in the eyes of God enabled men to look forward with hope to the good life after death in the Heavenly City. Meantime, the secular intellectual revolution, centering in the matter-of-fact study of history and science, gradually emancipated the minds of men from resignation to fate and the angry gods. Accumulated knowledge of history, filling in time past with a continuous succession of credible events, banished all lost golden ages to the realm of myth, and enabled men to live without distress in a changing world since it could be regarded as not necessarily changing for the worse. At the same time, a more competent observation and measurement of the action of material things disclosed an outer world of nature, indifferent to man indeed, yet behaving, not as the unpredictable sport of the gods, but in ways understandable to human reason and therefore ultimately subject to man's control.

Thus the conditions were fulfilled which made it possible for men to conceive of Utopia, neither as a lost golden age of the past nor as a Heavenly City after death prepared by the gods for the virtuous, but as a future state on earth of man's own devising. In a world of nature that could be regarded as amenable to man's control, and in a world of changing social relations that need not be regarded as an inevitable decline and fall from original perfection, it was possible to formulate the modern doctrine of progress: the idea that, by deliberate intention and rational direction, men can set the terms and indefinitely improve the conditions of their mundane existence.

The eighteenth century was the moment in history when men first fully realized the engaging implications of this resplendent idea, the moment when, not yet having been brought to the harsh appraisal of experience, it could be accepted with unclouded optimism. Never had the universe seemed less mysterious, more open and visible, more eager to yield its secrets to common-sense questions. Never had the nature of man seemed less perverse, or the mind of man more pliable to the pressure of rational persuasion. The essential reason for this confident optimism is that the marvels of scientific discovery disclosed to the men of that time a God who still functioned but was no longer angry. God the Father could be conceived as a beneficent First Cause who, having performed his essential task of creation, had withdrawn from the affairs of men, leaving them competently prepared and fully instructed for the task of achieving their own salvation. In one tremendous sentence Rousseau expressed the eighteenth-century world view of the universe and man's place in it. "Is it simple," he exclaimed, "is it natural that God should have gone in search of Moses in order to speak to Jean Jacques Rousseau?"

God had indeed spoken to Rousseau, he had spoken to all men, but his revelation was contained, not in Holy Writ interpreted by Holy Church, but in the great Book of Nature which was open for all men to read. To this open book of nature men would go when they wanted to know what God had said to them. Here they would find recorded the laws of nature and of nature's God, disclosing a universe constructed according to a rational plan; and that men might read these laws aright they had been endowed with reason, a bit of the universal intelligence placed within the individual to make manifest to him the universal reason implicit in things and events. "Natural law," as Volney so clearly and confidently put it, "is the regular and constant order of facts by which God rules the universe; the order which his wisdom presents to the sense and reason of men, to serve them as an equal and common rule of conduct, and to guide them, without distinction of race or sect, toward perfection and happiness." Thus God had devised a planned economy, and had endowed men with the capacity for managing it: to bring his ideas, his conduct, and his institutions into harmony with the universal laws of nature was man's simple allotted task.

At all times political theory must accommodate itself in some fashion to the prevailing world view, and liberal-democratic political theory was no exception to this rule. From time immemorial authority and obedience had been the cardinal concepts both of the prevailing world view and of political and social theory. From time immemorial men had been regarded as subject to overruling authority—the authority of the gods, and the authority of kings who were themselves gods, or descended from gods, or endowed with divine authority to rule in place of gods; and from time immemorial obedience to such divine authority was thought to be the primary obligation of men. Even the Greeks, who were so little afraid of their gods that they could hobnob with them in the most friendly and engaging way, re-

garded mortals as subject to them; and when they
lost faith in the gods they deified the state as the
highest good and subordinated the individual to
it. But the eighteenth-century world view, making
man the measure of all things, mitigated if it did
not destroy this sharp contrast between authority
and obedience. God still reigned but he did not
govern. He had, so to speak, granted his subjects
a constitution and authorized them to interpret
it as they would in the supreme court of reason.
Men were still subject to an overruling authority,
but the subjection could be regarded as voluntary
because self-imposed, and self-imposed because
obedience was exacted by nothing more oppres-
sive than their own rational intelligence.

Liberal-democratic political theory readily ac-
commodated itself to this change in the world
view. The voice of the people was now identified
with the voice of God, and all authority was derived from it. The individual instead of the state
or the prince was now deified and endowed with
imprescriptible rights, and since ignorance or
neglect of the rights of man was the chief cause
of social evils, the first task of political science
was to define these rights, the second to devise a
form of government suited to guarantee them.
The imprescriptible rights of man were easily
defined, since they were self-evident: "All men

are created equal, [and] are endowed by their Creator with certain inalienable rights, among which are life, liberty, and the pursuit of happiness." From this it followed that all just governments would remove those artificial restraints which impaired these rights, thereby liberating those natural impulses with which God had endowed the individual as a guide to thought and conduct. In the intellectual realm, freedom of thought and the competition of diverse opinion would disclose the truth, which all men, being rational creatures, would progressively recognize and willingly follow. In the economic realm, freedom of enterprise would disclose the natural aptitudes of each individual, and the ensuing competition of interests would stimulate effort, and thereby result in the maximum of material advantage for all. Liberty of the individual from social constraint thus turned out to be not only an inherent natural right but also a preordained natural mechanism for bringing about the material and moral progress of mankind. Men had only to follow reason and self-interest: something not themselves, God and Nature, would do whatever else was necessary for righteousness.

Thus modern liberal-democracy is associated with an ideology which rests upon something more than the minimum assumptions essential to any democratic government. It rests upon a philosophy of universally valid ends and means. Its fundamental assumption is the worth and dignity and creative capacity of the individual, so that the chief aim of government is the maximum of individual self-direction, the chief means to that end the minimum of compulsion by the state. Ideally considered, means and ends are conjoined in the concept of freedom: freedom of thought, so that the truth may prevail; freedom of occupation, so that careers may be open to talent; freedom of self-government, so that no one may be compelled against his will.

In the possibility of realizing this ideal the prophets and protagonists of democracy exhibited an unquestioned faith. If their faith seems to us somewhat naïve, the reason is that they placed a far greater reliance upon the immediate influence of good will and rational discussion in shaping the conduct of men than it is possible for us to do. This difference can be conveniently noted in a passage from the *Autobiography* of John Stuart Mill, in which he describes his father's extraordinary faith in two things—representative government and complete freedom of discussion.

So complete was my father's reliance on the influence of reason over the minds of mankind, whenever it was allowed to reach them, that he felt as if all would be gained if the whole population were taught to read, if all sorts of opinions were allowed to be addressed to them by word and writing, and if by means of the suffrage they could nominate a legislature to give effect to the opinions they adopted. He thought that when the legislature no longer represented a class interest, it would aim at the general interest, honestly and with adequate wisdom; since the people would be sufficiently under the guidance of educated intelligence, to make in general good choice of persons to represent them, and having done so to leave to those whom they had chosen a liberal discretion. Accordingly, aristocratic rule, the government of the few in any of its shapes, being in his eyes the only thing that stood between mankind and the administration of its affairs by the best wisdom to be found amongst them, was the object of his sternest disapprobation, and a democratic suffrage the principle article of his political creed.[1]

The beliefs of James Mill were shared by the little group of Philosophical Radicals who gathered about him. They were, indeed, the beliefs of all those who in the great crusading days placed their hopes in democratic government as a panacea for injustice and oppression. The actual working of democratic government, as these devoted

1. *Autobiography* (Columbia Press, 1924), p. 74.

enthusiasts foresaw it, the motives that would inspire men and the objects they would pursue in that ideal democracy which so many honest men have cherished and fought for, have never been better described than by James Bryce in his *Modern Democracies*. In this ideal democracy, says Bryce,

the average citizen will give close and constant attention to public affairs, recognizing that this is his interest as well as his duty. He will try to comprehend the main issues of policy, bringing to them an independent and impartial mind, which thinks first not of its own but of the general interest. If, owing to inevitable differences of opinion as to what are the measures needed for the general welfare, parties become inevitable, he will join one, and attend its meetings, but will repress the impulses of party spirit. Never failing to come to the polls, he will vote for his party candidate only if satisfied by his capacity and honesty. He will be ready to . . . be put forward as a candidate for the legislature (if satisfied of his own competence), because public service is recognized as a duty. With such citizens as electors, the legislature will be composed of upright and capable men, single-minded in their wish to serve the nation. Bribery in constituencies, corruption among public servants, will have disappeared. Leaders may not always be single-minded, nor assemblies always wise, nor administrators efficient, but all will be at any rate honest and zealous, so that an atmosphere of confidence and good will will prevail. Most of the causes that make for strife will be absent, for there will be no privileges, no advantages to excite jealousy. Office will be sought only because it gives opportunity for useful public service. Power will be shared by all, and a career open to all alike. Even if the law does not—perhaps it cannot—prevent the accumulation of fortunes, these will be few and not inordinate, for public vigilance will close the illegitimate paths to wealth. All but the most depraved persons will obey and support the law, feeling it to be their own. There will be no excuse for violence, because the constitution will provide a remedy for every grievance. Equality will produce a sense of human solidarity, will refine manners, and increase brotherly kindness.[2]

Such is the ideal form of modern democracy laid away in heaven. I do not need to tell you that its earthly counterpart resembles it but slightly. In the next lecture I shall discuss some of the circumstances that brought about so flagrant a discord between democracy as it was ideally projected and democracy as it actually functions today.

2. I, 48.

II

THE REALITY

Men mistook the pernicious channels in which selfish propensities had been flowing for the propensities themselves, which were sure to find new channels when the old had been destroyed.

JAMES BRYCE

Those who own the country ought to govern it.

JOHN JAY

I

IN the preceding lecture we were concerned with the ideal form of democracy. It is obvious that the reality does not strictly conform to this ideal. There is nothing remarkable in that. The ideal is always better than the real—otherwise there would be no need for ideals. We have been told, as if it were a surprising thing, that in Russia the Revolution has been betrayed. But it was bound to be betrayed. It is in the nature of revolutions to be betrayed, since life and history have an inveterate habit of betraying the ideal aspirations of men. In this sense the liberal-democratic revolution was likewise bound to be betrayed—men were sure to be neither so rational nor so well-intentioned as the ideology conceived them to be. But while a little betrayal is a normal thing, too much is something that calls for explanation. The liberal-democratic revolution has been so far betrayed, the ideal so imperfectly portrayed in the course of events, that its characteristic features cannot easily be recognized in any democratic society today. In this lecture I shall attempt to disclose some of the essential reasons for the profound discord between democracy as it was ideally projected and democracy as a going concern.

Stated in general terms the essential reason is that the idea of liberty, as formulated in the eighteenth century, although valid enough for that time, has in one fundamental respect ceased to be applicable to the situation in which we find ourselves. In the eighteenth century the most obvious oppressions from which men suffered derived from governmental restraints on the free activity of the individual. Liberty was therefore naturally conceived in terms of the emancipation of the individual from such restraints. In the economic realm this meant the elimination of governmental restraints on the individual in choosing his occupation, in contracting for the acquisition and disposal of property, and the purchase and sale of personal services. But in our time, as a result of the growing complexities of a technological society, the emancipation of the individual from governmental restraint in his economic activities has created new oppressions, so that for the majority of men liberty can be achieved only by an extension of governmental regulation of competitive business enterprise. It is in the economic realm that the traditional idea of liberty is no longer applicable; in the economic realm, accordingly, that the discord between

34

democracy as an ideal and democracy as a going concern is most flagrant, most disillusioning, and most dangerous.

In order to elaborate this statement it will be well, first of all, to note the chief characteristics of the social situation in the eighteenth century— the situation against which the liberal-democratic revolution was directed, and from which the eighteenth-century conception of liberty emerged as an obvious and valid rationalization.

From the twelfth to the seventeenth century the cardinal economic fact in western Europe was the rise of an industrial capitalist class in the towns; the cardinal political fact was the consolidation of royal power over all classes and corporations within definite territorial limits. The chief obstacles encountered by kings in this political process were two: first, the feudal vassals who claimed, and often exercised, virtual independence within their domains; second, the Roman Church, which claimed to be superior to the civil power, was in large part a self-governing institution, and exercised in fact over the king's subjects an authority independent of, and often in conflict with, the authority of the king.

In this three-cornered struggle for power, kings were sometimes supported by the church against the nobles, sometimes by the nobles against the church; but the persistent and effective support against both church and nobility came from the rising industrial class. Merchants and traders always found the turbulence of the nobility bad for business, and were usually willing, however painful it may have been, to supply the king with some of the money he needed to establish orderly government. Thus in the course of centuries, chiefly with the aid of the industrial bourgeois class, kings gradually reduced the nobles to the status of landed proprietors who retained, as the price of submission, the distinctions and prerogatives of a superior social class.

Meantime, the long struggle for the subordination of the church to royal power was virtually completed by the upheaval known as the Protestant Reformation, and it was the growing power and heretical ideas of the industrial classes that made the Reformation successful. Everywhere stronger in the towns than in the country, stronger in industrialized than in nonindustrialized countries, the Protestant Reformation was in effect a revolt of the middle classes against a church which, being controlled by a landed aristocracy, enforced ethical standards and religious practices unsuited to the temper and contrary to the interests of an industrial society. The chief political result of the Reformation was that by

36

breaking the power of Rome it enhanced the power of kings, and by enhancing the power of kings it subordinated the church to the state, and thereby reduced the clergy, like the nobility, to the status of a privileged social class.

Thus in the seventeenth century, as a result of the rise of an industrial capitalist class, the consolidation of royal power, and the survival of nobles and clergy as privileged classes within the state, there emerged in western Europe a social system that was everywhere much the same. The prevailing form of government was absolute monarchy. In theory the power of the king rested upon the doctrine of divine right, supplemented by the Roman Law precept "What the Prince wills has the force of law." In practice the power of the king rested upon the support of nobles, clergy, and the rich bourgeois industrialists and financiers, and functioned for the most part to their advantage by exploiting an underlying population of peasants and workers.

It was what we should call a highly regimented system—a system in which the rights and obligations of the individual, always subject to the arbitrary will of the king, were normally determined by the rights and obligations appertaining to the class in which he was born. Generally speaking, there was for the individual neither freedom of occupation, nor of opinion or religion, nor any recognized method by which he might initiate or modify the law and custom by which his thought and conduct were controlled. The character of the liberal-democratic revolution which occurred from the seventeenth to the nineteenth centuries was conditioned by this fact. Dispensing with verbal refinements, all revolutions are made in behalf of liberty—freedom from some sort of real or fancied oppression; and in a social situation in which the individual was so obviously restrained and oppressed by law and custom not of his own making, it was inevitable that liberty should be conceived in terms of the emancipation of the individual from social and political control.

The revolution was initiated and directed, not by those who were most oppressed, but by those who were most aware of oppression and most competent to denounce and resist it—that is to say, not by the brutalized and ignorant peasants and workers, but by the educated and well-to-do middle classes. The bourgeoisie derived their power neither from birth nor office, but from money, that abstract and supple measure of the material value of all things. They acquired the education, cultivated the virtues, and developed the mentality appropriate to the occupations that engaged them. Occupied with practical affairs,

with defined and determinable relations, with
concrete things and their disposal and calculable
cash value, they cultivated the virtues of thrift
and prudence, dependability and sound judgment, and developed a pragmatic and skeptical
temper, averse to the mystical and other-worldly,
little disposed to slavish adherence to tradition,
easily adaptable to the new and the experimental.

In every country the liberal-democratic revolution developed, with occasional violent up-
heavals, in the measure that the bourgeoisie acquired power and became class conscious—
became aware, that is to say, of their peculiar
class interests and virtues; and of the frustration
of their interests and virtues by rococo class distinctions, and by arbitrary royal decrees which
hampered business enterprise and deprived them
of their property for the benefit of an aristocracy
which they regarded as less intelligent, less moral,
and less socially useful than themselves. The
central, dramatic episode in the rise of liberal-
democracy was the French Revolution; and it was
in connection with this episode that there appeared in western Europe an exceptionally able
group of intellectuals who rationalized the social
situation by identifying the middle-class interests
and virtues with the rights of all men—the right
of all men to equality of status and of oppor-

39

tunity, to freedom of occupation and of economic enterprise, to freedom of opinion and of religion, and to freedom from arbitrary political authority.

II

FORTUNATELY for the bourgeoisie and for the revolution, the interests of the middle classes were, in one respect, identical with the interests of the great majority. The liberal-democratic revolution could not have been won if it had been fought on behalf of bourgeois class interests alone. Of all the liberties demanded, freedom of economic enterprise was the one least stressed by the Philosophers and of least importance for the purposes of revolutionary propaganda. The liberty which could be demanded with most assurance and denied with least grace was liberty of person and of opinion—freedom of religion, freedom of speech and the press, freedom of learning and of teaching, freedom from the insane brutalities practiced in the civil and ecclesiastical adminis- tration of justice and in the punishment of crimes. In proclaiming the worth and dignity of the individual, in demanding the emancipation of men from the inhumanity of man to man, the bourgeois spokesmen were appealing to interests transcending all class lines. They were appealing to the spirit of Christianity against its practices, and espousing the cause with which all the saints and sages of the world had been identified. In doing so they injected into the liberal-democratic revolution the quality of a religious crusade, and thereby enlisted the wide-spread support which alone could assure its success.

The political and economic interests of the bourgeoisie could not, unfortunately, be thus identified with the interests of all. On the contrary, the interests of the bourgeoisie, both in the political and the economic realm, proved in the long run to be in sharp conflict with the interests of the masses. It was the interest of the bourgeoisie to deny to the masses the political privileges which they demanded for themselves; while the freedom of economic enterprise which enriched bourgeois employers turned out to be, for the proletarian peasants and workers, no more than the old subjection under new forms. As liberal-democracy emerged into the light of day, this conflict of class interests became more obvious and more disastrous; and it is this conflict which in our time has created those profound social discords which so largely nullify the theory and threaten to undermine the stability of democratic institutions.

In the earlier stages of the revolution, when the chief task was to deprive kings and aristocrats of political power and social privilege, this latent conflict between middle- and lower-class interests was not apparent. For the time being, indeed, it did not exist. The tyranny of kings and aristocrats, so effectively denounced by the Philosophers, was real enough, and so long as it existed all the unprivileged, bourgeois and people alike, had a common interest in resisting it. The doctrine that all men had a natural right to govern themselves seemed then but a simple truth, and the bourgeoisie could accept it without bothering too much about its practical application, all the more so since only by accepting it could they enlist the support of the people in destroying absolute monarchy and class privilege. In all the great "revolutionary days"—the English civil wars in the seventeenth century, the American and the French revolutions at the close of the eighteenth, the South American wars of independence, the revolutions of 1830 and 1848—in all these crucial struggles in which the tyranny of kings and aristocrats was still the central issue, the bourgeoisie and the people are found united in the effort to win political freedom by overthrowing the existing regime. They differed only in the respective parts which they played in the struggle: the function of the bourgeoisie was to take the initiative and supply the ideas; the function of the people was to erect the barricades and supply the necessary force.

It is always easier for diverse groups to unite for the destruction of an existing regime than it is to unite for the construction of a new one. Having united to destroy the tyranny of kings and aristocrats, the bourgeoisie and the people were divided on the question of what political liberty should mean in practice. The doctrine that all men had a natural right to govern themselves was interpreted by the people to mean that all adult male citizens should share in choosing the magistrates and shaping the laws by which the community was governed. By the bourgeoisie it was interpreted to mean, as John Jay put it, that "those who own the country ought to govern it." In this respect the first result of the revolution was everywhere essentially a victory for the bourgeoisie. Kings lost their absolute power, aristocrats lost their special privileges, or most of them; but political liberty—the right to choose the magistrates and enact the laws by which the community was governed—was limited to the people of property; the masses, having served their purpose by erecting the barricades, found themselves still excluded from what Guizot called "the political country."

Having thus, with the aid of the people, elbowed kings and aristocrats out of the seats of power, the bourgeoisie promptly united with the aristocrats to control the state. They had a common interest in excluding the people from political privilege, but in the competition for votes and power within the political country their interests were opposed. There accordingly emerged, for the promotion of their respective interests, two political parties which, although known by different names in different countries, we may call conservative and liberal. Conservative parties were composed for the most part of the landed aristocracy, the clergy of the established churches, high-placed bureaucrats, and hangers-on of royal courts. In some countries, more royalist than the king, they at first entertained the vain hope of restoring the ancient regime; but in any case they defended the interests of land against capital, the established church against dissenting religions, and old social distinctions and aristocratic prestige against the leveling influence of democratic customs. Liberal parties were composed of the educated and well-to-do middle classes—businessmen, professional people, middle-class intellectuals, perhaps a few liberalized aristocrats. Occupying a middle position, the liberal parties fought on two fronts: equally opposed to absolutism and democracy, they were defenders of liberty against kings and

aristocrats, but defenders of their own newly acquired privilege against the people.

In this situation, there emerged a third political
party—variously called republican, progressive
liberal, radical—which for convenience we may
call democratic. The democratic party represented
those who were still excluded from the political
country—at first more particularly the industrial
workers, who were most oppressed and the first
to become class conscious. They were commonly
led by middle-class intellectuals who formulated
for them a doctrine and a program. The doctrine
was the pure liberal-democratic ideology which
middle-class liberals professed in theory but denied in practice—the doctrine that all men had a
natural right to govern themselves; and the chief
point in the program was accordingly the extension of the suffrage to all adult male citizens, in
the confident belief that the workers, once possessed of the right to vote for those who made the
laws, could correct by legislation the economic
inequalities that oppressed them.

In the course of time, after much fruitless effort
and some abortive uprisings, the people were admitted to the political country—in the United
States during the period from about 1830 to 1840,
in European countries for the most part during
the last three decades of the century. To this re-

sult both logic and political tactics contributed. In point of logic, it was difficult for middle-class Liberals, who had won political privilege by advocating the right of all men to govern themselves, to refute the argument that the masses as well as the classes should enjoy that right. But it was less the logic of the ideology than of political strategy that determined the outcome. As the fear of kings declined and the revolution was accepted as an accomplished fact, the opposition between upper-class Liberal and Conservative parties declined also. Agreeing upon fundamentals, they were chiefly divided by the competitive struggle for votes; and it seemed obvious that the party which first pleased the masses by giving them the right to vote would stand the best chance of winning their support at the polls. Generally speaking, therefore, at least so far as European countries are concerned, it can hardly be said that the people forced their way into the political country. Quite as often as not they were admitted by Conservative or Liberal party governments, each of which, in the particular instance, hoped to increase its voting strength by enlarging the electorate.

The adoption of universal manhood suffrage was thought at the time to be a signal triumph for democracy. And it did in fact add something to the power of the people, since it compelled upper-class parties to take account of popular opinion in formulating policies and devising measures that would appeal to the mass of the voters. But on the whole, the admission of the people to the political country did very little to increase their power or improve the conditions under which they lived. Political control remained, as before, essentially in the hands of upper-class political parties.

Many reasons may be advanced for the failure of the people to profit by their apparent victory. When they entered the political country they found the upper classes intrenched in all the strategic positions. The forms and procedure of representative institutions were already established; political parties, representing for the most part the upper classes, were well organized; and the technique for selecting candidates and manipulating elections was such that politics was a profession only men of property and social position could enter with much chance of success. In theory the masses were free to present to the electorate the measures that seemed to them desirable for the public good; in fact the means of propaganda were freely available only to the educated and well-to-do. In theory the poor man could vote for candidates of his own choosing; in fact his choice was limited to candidates who represented the dominant upper-class parties. It is true that in the course

47

of time the people organized working-class socialist parties of their own; but while such parties
often obtained from conservative or liberal governments measures designed to protect the interests
of the poor, effective political control still remained in the hands of those who could easily af-
ford the expensive luxury of self-government.

These are the superficial reasons for the failure
of political equality to safeguard the interests of
the people. The more fundamental reason is to be
found in the economic structure of the society
that emerged from the liberal-democratic revolution. Individual liberty in the political realm
proved inadequate because individual liberty in
the economic realm failed to bring about even that
minimum degree of equality of possessions and of
opportunity without which political equality is
scarcely more than an empty form. This point,
since it is fundamental, calls for some elaboration.

III

THE principle of individual freedom in the economic realm, although not much stressed in the
propaganda of the great crusading days, was always an integral part of the liberal-democratic
ideology. For the needed emancipation of indus-
try from the hampering restraints of monopolistic

48

privilege and petty governmental regulation, it was a sound working principle; but applied without qualifications it could only benefit the industrial bourgeoisie at the expense of the underlying population of peasants and workers. As set forth in the *Wealth of Nations*, and in the more rigorous and apparently more scientific works of the English classical economists, the principle was indeed scarcely more than pure rationalization of the business interests of capitalist employers; but this ominous fact was long concealed because the principle was formulated in terms of the word liberty, the magic of which was sufficient at that time to give a general sanction even to the brutalities of cut-throat competition and the systematic degradation of women and children. The present misery of the workers could be more easily contemplated and dismissed because it could be regarded as a necessary but temporary phase in the operation of a divinely ordained law of progress. The average humane middle-class man, whether employer or not, could therefore accept the principle of individual freedom in the economic realm, along with the other great freedoms, since it so happily enabled him to reconcile his selfish with his altruistic impulses by assuring him that he could best serve God and his neighbor by doing as he pleased. "Private advantage a public benefit"—such was

49

the succinct formula by which the prosperous middle classes justified their amiable expectation that when everyone was free all would presently be equal, when all were equal everyone would presently have enough, when all had enough no one would any longer be unjust or inhumane.

The expectation was surely naïve, in no sort of harmony with the relevant facts of social experience. Even under the most favorable circumstances, a society of uprooted and freely competing individuals must have functioned to the advantage of the few who by good fortune, intelligence, or lack of scruple were able to acquire wealth and employ it to advance their interests through the mechanism of politics: the times would always be ripe for a sufficient number of not-too-good men to come to the aid of the party. But this result was greatly accelerated and intensified by those changes in the economic and material conditions of life which, effected without blare of trumpets and scarcely perceived at the time, are now known as the industrial or technological revolution of modern times.

Technological is the better term. Industrial is wholly inadequate to denote one of the two or three major revolutions in the history of the human race. Man is a tool-using animal, and all civilization is conditioned by the sources of natural

power known to him and the mechanical appliances he can invent to make such power available
for use. The first great epoch of discovery and
invention takes us back before the time of recorded
history. All the more obvious sources of natural
power—gravitation, fire, wind and water, do-
mesticated animals, the fertility of the soil—and
the simple hand tools, weapons, utensils, and appliances for making such power available were
known to primitive man. From the time of the invention of writing, some five or six thousand years
ago, until comparatively recent times few if any
new sources of natural power, except crude explo-
sives and magnetic force, were discovered; and
during all that long time the mechanical appliances available, although more numerous and
greatly perfected, were essentially of the same order as those employed from time immemorial.

But we are now living in the second great epoch
of discovery and invention. Since the seventeenth
century, the discovery of steam power, gas, elec-
tricity, and radiation have made possible those
innumerable tools and appliances, those complicated and powerful machines, and those delicate
instruments of precision which elicit our wonder
and our admiration. The result has been that the
new technology, by giving men unprecedented
control over material things, has transformed the

relatively simple agricultural communities of the eighteenth century into societies far more complex and impersonal than anything the prophets of liberal-democracy could have imagined—mechanized Leviathans which Thomas Jefferson at least would have regarded as unreal and fantastic and altogether unsuited to the principles of liberty and equality as he understood them.

I need not say that the influence of the technological revolution has not been confined to any particular aspect of social life. On the contrary, it has exerted and still exerts a decisive influence in modifying all the habitual patterns of thought and conduct. But I am here concerned with the influence of the technological revolution in accelerating and intensifying that concentration of wealth and power in the hands of a few which the principles of individual freedom in the economic realm would in any case have tended to bring about.

The first and most obvious result of the technological revolution has been to increase the amount of wealth in the form of material things which can be produced in a given time by a given population. For example, in 1913 there was produced in Great Britain seven billion yards of cotton cloth for export alone. In 1750 the total population of Great Britain, working with the mechanical appliances then available, could have produced only a small fraction of that amount. A second result of the technological revolution is that, as machines are perfected and become more automatic, man power plays a relatively less important part in the production of a given amount of wealth in a given time. Fifty years ago, when all type was set by hand, the labor of several men was required to print, fold, and arrange in piles the signatures of a book. Today machines can do it all, and far more rapidly; little man power is required, except that a mechanic, who may pass the time sitting in a chair, must be present in case anything goes wrong with the machine. And finally, a third result of the technological revolution is that, under the system of private property in the means of production and the price system as a method of distributing wealth, the greater part of the wealth produced, since it is produced by the machines, goes to those who own or control the machines, while those who work the machines receive that part only which can be exacted by selling their services in a market where wages are impersonally adjusted to the necessities of the machine process.

I use the phrase "own or control the machines" for the reason that, as a result of modern technology and business organization, those who own private property in the means of production do not necessarily control it. The ownership of property is now a highly intangible and illusive concept. Mass production calls for enormous industrial plants which are commonly managed by corporations and financed by selling corporation stock to the investing public. If I buy ten shares of General Motors I may be said to own that amount of General Motors property, but I have no control of it. The property is controlled by those who own a majority of the stock, and the majority of the stock is commonly owned by a few persons. Ownership, as far as I am concerned, consists in the possession of a slip of paper which gives me a lively hope that those who control the property will periodically send me a check for a certain sum of money: if they fail to do so there is nothing I can do about it. By the intricate device of the holding company, control may be still further concentrated and still further divorced from ownership: several corporations may be controlled by a few persons who have little or no interest in the operating companies except to manipulate and exploit them for financial gain. Thus it happens that while the ownership of private property in the means of production may be widely distributed, the effective control of that property is likely to be concentrated in the hands of a few.

If the concept of ownership is intangible and

illusive, the concept of property is no less so. The value of General Motors property resides, not in the physical plant and the financial assets alone, but essentially in the business as a going concern. To be a prosperous going concern, the corporation must be able to purchase labor and supplies at a cost that will enable it to sell its products throughout the entire community at a profit. For this reason General Motors cannot live or die to itself alone. Its prosperity, and therefore the value of its property, conditions and is conditioned by the prosperity of innumerable individuals and business enterprises—the enterprises, large and small throughout the community and even throughout the world, which sell its cars and supply it with raw material, fuel, and equipment; the individuals who, as laborers or stockholders, are associated with General Motors and with the many enterprises that are integrated with it.

The value of private property in the means of production is thus not a private matter. It is both cause and effect in the functioning of a highly integrated and delicately adjusted industrial structure that touches the public interest at every point. That the few who control private property in the means of production should be wealthy men is no great matter. What matters is that their control of the means of production gives them an indeterminate and impersonal power over the lives and fortunes of millions of people unknown to them —power which they are sometimes unwilling but far more often quite unable to use for the public good.

In any society there is bound to be a close connection between economic and political power. In any society those who possess economic power, like other people, are disposed to identify their economic interests with the general good, and to promote their interests through the mechanism of politics and propaganda. But in modern industrial societies, based upon democratic political control and the principle of free economic enterprise, the beneficiaries of private property in the means of production are in a peculiarly advantageous position for molding opinion and shaping legislation. Their advantage arises less from the fact that they can and do spend money freely for those purposes, than from the fact that political procedure and the instruments of propaganda are so integrated with the industrial system that legislation and opinion more or less automatically respond to the pressure of the system of free enterprise from which their economic power is derived.

In democratic societies political power is mediated through political parties organized primarily for the purpose of obtaining control of the govern-

ment by winning elections. To win elections a
political party must of course formulate a program
of legislation that will appeal to the voters. But
elections are not won on the merits of a program
alone. The winning of an election is a practical
business enterprise, which calls for a capital in-
vestment in the form of a campaign fund, and for
an intricate organization of employees—a political machine managed by professional politicians
whose business it is to deliver the vote. Contributions to the campaign fund may be made from
interested or disinterested motives; but the largest
contributions will commonly be made by wealthy
men or corporations expecting in return that the
party will not, at the very least, be altogether indifferent to the kind of legislation they desire.

The professional politician, whose business it
is to deliver the vote, is concerned primarily with
the vote of those whose loyalty to the party is determined less by the merits of the party program
than by the disposition of the party to confer
tangible benefits upon them. The function of the
highest species of politician is to handle the pa-
tronage, to distribute appointive offices to those
who can best serve the party. The function of the
lowest species of politician—the *déclassé* ward
healer—is to do what respectable statesmen know
must be done but are prevented by the mores from

doing themselves, namely, to see to it that the poor and dispossessed are provided with a minimum of subsistence, and not too much hampered in their private enterprises, even sometimes if they happen to be on the wrong side of the fence, by the majesty of the law. In delivering the vote, the ward healer is the henchman of the political boss, the political boss has the necessary contacts with the party leaders who hold elective or appointive offices, and the political leaders have the necessary personal and social contacts with the businessmen who contribute so generously to the campaign fund. In every community, large or small, there is this unavowed, undercover integration of economic and political power; and apart from some unanticipated ethical disturbance in the climate of opinion, legislation, always defended by statesmen in terms of the common good, is always insensibly influenced by the pressure of the predominant industrial interest.

In molding opinion, no less than in shaping legislation, those who possess economic power have a great advantage over the general run of citizens. This is not to say that freedom of speech and the press does not exist in democratic societies. One has only to compare nondemocratic with democratic societies to realize that, in a very real and important sense, it does exist. In democratic societies any man may freely express his opinion without first looking furtively over his shoulder to see if a government spy is in the offing; any man may publish a book or a newspaper without first submitting it to an official censor. This is the fundamentally important privilege; and no cataloguing of incidental violations of civil liberties, serious and deplorable as they are, can obscure the fact that through the press and the radio detailed information about events, and the most diverse opinions, are with little let or hindrance daily and hourly presented to the people.

Nevertheless, the average individual, although free to express his ideas, plays a distinctly minor role in the molding of opinion: his role is not to initiate, but passively to receive information and ideas presented to him by others. The propaganda of social or political opinion, to be effective under modern conditions, must be organized; and its promoters will have an indifferent success unless they resort to mass production and distribution of their wares. The chief instruments of propaganda—the press and broadcasting stations—are not readily available to the average individual for conveying his ideas: they can be effectively used only by the government, political parties and party leaders, prominent organizations, wealthy men and business corporations, associations organized for specific purposes, and the writers of books which publishing houses find it worth while to publish.

Even more important is the fact that the instruments of propaganda are themselves business corporations organized and financed for profit, and as such subject to those influences that condition and are conditioned by the system of free economic enterprise. Newspapers are free to print all the news that's fit to print; but they cannot consistently propagate ideas that will alienate the business interests whose paid advertisements enable them to distribute profits to the stockholders. Broadcasting corporations are free from government censorship, or reasonably so, reasonably free to broadcast what they will; but in the last analysis they will not broadcast that which seriously offends the prevailing mores, or the business enterprises which, in this country at least, sponsor and finance their programs of entertainment. In democratic societies free and impartial discussion, from which the truth is supposed to emerge, is permitted and does occur. But the thinking of the average man is largely shaped by a wealth of factual information and the conflicting opinions which the selective process of competitive business enterprise presents to him for consideration: information, the truth of which he cannot verify; ideas,

formulated by persons he does not know, and to
often inspired by private economic interests th..
are never avowed.

Such, in broad outline, are the circumstances
that may serve to explain the profound discord
between democracy as an ideal and as a reality. In
terms of the ideal there should have emerged from
the liberal-democratic revolution a relatively simple society of free, equal, and prosperous citizens,
fraternally coöperating to effect, by rational discussion and mutual concession, the common good.
In fact there emerged an extremely complex society in which highly intricate and impersonal
economic forces, stronger than good will or deliberate intention or rational direction, brought
about an increasing concentration of wealth and
power in the hands of the fortunate few, and
thereby nullified, for the majority of the people,
many of those essential liberties which provide
both the theoretical justification and the necessary
conditions for the practical success of democratic
institutions.

This discord, long since perceived by the dis-
cerning, has in our time become so flagrant that
in many countries the ideal has been abandoned
as an illusion. In these countries new social philos-
ophies now prevail which maintain that the attempt to apply the principles of individual liberty,

not only in the economic but in the political and the intellectual realm, was a fundamental error, and is responsible for the social and international conflicts which now bewilder and distress the world.

To accept this view implies the end of democratic institutions as we know them, and the renunciation of that faith in the worth and dignity of the individual which we have cherished even if we have not always justified it in action. I do not accept this view. I believe that in the long run it will prove mistaken—fatal to any way of life that can rightly be called civilized. But I also believe that if the democratic way of life is to survive we must give to the traditional concept of freedom a more positive content. The traditional concept of individual liberty is essentially negative. The freedom it emphasizes is freedom from constraint, and indeed from a particular kind of constraint, that is to say, governmental constraint. In the economic realm the result of freeing the individual from governmental constraint is that today far too many people are always in danger of losing those positive goods without which freedom from governmental constraint is of no value. What the average man now needs is the opportunity to acquire by his own effort, in an occupation for which he is fitted, the economic security which is essen-

62

tial to decent and independent living. This opportunity has now disappeared for something like a quarter of the working population. In my opinion it can only be restored, if at all, by such governmental regulations of our economy as may be necessary to enable private economic enterprise to function effectively and for the common good.

If then the democratic way of life is to survive we must distinguish the kinds of individual freedom that are essential to it from those that are unessential or disastrous. Broadly speaking, the kinds that are essential are those which the individual enjoys in his intellectual and political activities; the kinds that are unessential are the relatively unrestrained liberties he has hitherto enjoyed in his economic activities. The distinction is comparatively easy to make in theory, but will be extremely difficult to effect in practice. Not the least of the difficulties arises from the fact that in the traditional ideology the freedom of the individual in the political, the intellectual, and the economic realms are so intimately associated that they seem to stand or fall together. The result is that any proposal to regulate by governmental authority the system of free economic enterprise is sure to be opposed on the ground that if the system of free economic enterprise cannot be maintained the other freedoms of democracy, freedom of thought and political freedom, must in the end be abandoned also. Whether this is true can only be determined by the event. Whatever the event may be, the difficult but essential task which confronts all democratic societies today may be formulated as follows: how in practice to curtail the freedom of the individual in economic enterprise sufficiently to effect that equality of opportunity and of possessions without which democracy is an empty form, and at the same time to preserve that measure of individual freedom in intellectual and political life without which it cannot exist. Some aspects of this problem will be considered in the final lecture.

III

THE DILEMMA

Blight—not on the grain!
Drouth—not in the springs!
Rot—not from the rain!

What shadow hidden or
Unseen hand in our midst
Ceaselessly touches our faces?
ARCHIBALD MACLEISH

THE problem of modern democracies as I have just defined it may be otherwise stated: Can the flagrant inequality of possessions and of opportunity now existing in democratic societies be corrected by the democratic method? If it cannot be so corrected the resulting discontent and confusion will be certain, sooner or later, to issue in some form of revolutionary or military dictatorship. This then is the dilemma which confronts democratic societies: to solve the economic problem by the democratic method, or to cease to be democratic societies.

It is obvious that the problem, intrinsically, is an economic one. At the present moment it takes the spectacular form of unemployment. For the past ten years, in the most prosperous democratic societies, from 10 to 20 per cent of the working population, for the most part willing but unable to find work, has been kept alive by public or private charity or by jobs created for that purpose by the government. Unemployment is no new thing, but never before in democratic societies has it reached the proportions of a major social catastrophe.

The catastrophe cannot be explained as an act of God, cannot be attributed to destructive natural forces beyond human control. The people are famished, but there is no famine. On the contrary, there is wealth in abundance, or should be. Given our natural resources, man power, and technical equipment, there could be produced, in this country at least, sufficient wealth to provide all the people with the necessities of life and many of the desired comforts and luxuries besides. Yet in spite of widespread and insistent human need, the technical equipment is used only in part, the man power is not fully employed. In a land of plenty millions are destitute. Obviously the situation is one which arises not from lack of potential wealth, but from some defect in the method of producing and distributing wealth. That the defect is a serious one is indicated by a simple, ironic fact—the fact that in a world in which millions are destitute it is thought necessary, and under the prevailing system of production and distribution of wealth apparently is so, to limit the production of the necessities of life in order to keep people from starving.

The prevailing system for the production and distribution of wealth is variously denoted by the phrases capitalist system, competitive system, price system, system of free enterprise, system of *laissez-faire*. Its theoretical justification derives from the general assumption of the liberal-demo-

cratic ideology—the assumption that social welfare can best be achieved by reducing governmental interference with the freedom of the individual to a minimum. The assumption was never
better stated than by John Stuart Mill in his famous essay *On Liberty*. Governmental interference with the activities of the individual, he maintained, is never justified except when manifestly
necessary to prevent the activities of some individuals from injuring others. The principle is
similarly, but more succinctly, formulated in the
French Declaration of the Rights of Man: "Liberty is the right of everyone to do whatever does
not injure others."

Applied to the economic realm, this principle
was interpreted to mean the maximum freedom
of the individual to choose his occupation or business, and to enter freely into contracts for the
acquisition or disposal of private property and for
the purchase or sale of personal services. It was
assumed that the free play of individual initiative,
stimulated by the acquisitive instinct, would result
in the maximum production of wealth, and that
the competitive instinct, operating through the
law of supply and demand and the resulting price
system, would result in as equitable a distribution
of wealth as the natural qualities and defects of
men would permit. In this system the function of

the government was reduced to defining and guaranteeing the rights of private property, enforcing the rules of contract, and preserving social order. Having defined the rules of the game, the government would see that they were enforced, but would not otherwise interfere with the players. Let the game go on and the best man win. *Laissez-faire, laissez-passer!*

Contrary to a wide-spread belief, *laissez-faire* was never more than a theory imperfectly applied. The happy, imagined time when government did not interfere in the freedom of the individual by meddling in business never in fact existed. The institution of private property is itself a most drastic regulation of business enterprise, the law of contract a fundamental interference with the liberty of the individual. But assuming private property and the law of contract as part of the system, there never was a time when government did not find it necessary, according to Mill's famous definition, to interfere with the activities of some individuals in order to prevent those activities from injuring others.

In England the trend toward *laissez-faire* was reversed before it was completed. A decade before 1846, when the doctrine was officially adopted by the repeal of the corn laws, the government had found it necessary to restrict free enterprise by

passing the first Factory Acts for the protection of
women and children. And from that day to this,
in England and in every industrialized country,
including the United States, the governmental
regulation of private property, of free competition
and free contract, of the price of commodities and
of labor, of the inheritance of property and of the
disposal of income from it, has steadily increased.
This extension of governmental regulation, this
trend toward what is called social legislation, was
brought about by the pressure of labor unions supported by the humane sentiment of the community, and underlying it is the assumption, avowed
or unavowed, that the system of *laissez-faire*, so
eminently successful in stimulating the production of wealth, is incapable, without governmental
regulation, of bringing about an equitable or even
a tolerable distribution of it. It is far too late to
ask whether government should interfere in business enterprise. It always has interfered in business
enterprise. The only relevant question is in what
ways and to what extent it should so interfere.

Nevertheless, in spite of increasing governmental regulation, the theory of *laissez-faire* was
never abandoned. The prevailing assumption was,
and still is in democratic societies, that governmental regulation should be kept to a minimum,
however high the minimum might in the event

prove to be. It was taken for granted that the basic right and the assured foundation of the economic structure of society was private property in the means of production, free enterprise, and the competitive system. Social legislation was regarded as no more than a limited, if necessary, concession to adverse circumstances, a series of minor adjustments that would leave the system intact while enhancing its efficiency. In the optimistic decade before the Great War, social legislation came to be widely regarded, indeed, as in some sense an integral part of the system of free enterprise, a kind of insurance against the subversive doctrine of Socialism, a preordained and peaceful means of transforming that anomaly of progress and poverty which Henry George had so graphically described into that progress and prosperity which the prophets of democracy had so confidently predicted.

Since the Great War faith in social legislation as a means of validating the system of free enterprise has been much impaired. Surveying the history of a century of governmental regulation of business enterprise, it is obvious that while regulation has done much to correct minor evils it has as yet failed to solve the fundamental problem of an equitable distribution of wealth. On the contrary, the problem of the distribution of wealth is more serious and more insistent now than it was in the time of Henry George, so much so, indeed, that if the anomaly of progress and poverty is less glaring than it was, the only reason is that while the poverty is more patent the progress is less assured.

Inevitably, therefore, the question, long since raised, becomes every day more insistent: Can the problem of the production and distribution of wealth be solved, within the framework of the existing system of private property and free enterprise, by any amount of governmental regulation? In short, are the defects of the system of private property in the means of production incidental or inherent?

II

That the defects of the capitalist system are inherent is the contention of those ideologies known as Socialism and Communism. Socialism and Communism, taken in the generic sense of the words, are at least as old as Plato; but in their modern forms they derive from the doctrines formulated by Karl Marx in the middle of the last century.

Marxian Socialism, inspired by the failure of democratic institutions to effect an equitable distribution of wealth, was essentially a reinterpretation of the modern doctrine of progress, and as such it comprised a social theory and a philosophy of history. As a social theory it maintained that the social structure at any time is fundamentally determined by the methods of production and distribution of wealth, and that the prevailing institutions and ideas are those best adapted to maintain the interests of the class which, by ownership and control of the chief forms of wealth, dominates the social structure in its own interest. As a philosophy of history it maintained that social change, or progress, is the result, not of a conflict of ideas, but of economic forces, a conflict between the economic interests of the ruling and the dispossessed classes. Not by the persuasive force of ideas, but only by the impersonal pressure of economic conditions, could the ruling class ever be dispossessed, or the institutions and ideas through which its power operates ever be transformed.

Applying this theory to European history, Marx found that the liberal-democratic revolution was the result of the conflict between the economic interests of the landed aristocracy and the rising capitalist class. So far from reflecting the triumph of true over false ideas, it reflected the triumph of capital over land as the predominant factor in production; and the superstructure of liberal-demo-

74

cratic ideas and institutions, so far from having a universal validity, had merely the relative and temporary value of being suited to the functioning of the capitalist system and the interests of the ruling bourgeois class. The liberal-democratic revolution could not, therefore, be regarded as the final term in the historic process. On the contrary, the capitalist system once established, there necessarily developed within it a new conflict between the interests of the ruling bourgeois class and the dispossessed proletariat which would inevitably issue in another social revolution.

The coming social revolution was inevitable, according to Marx, because the capitalist system, like the landed aristocratic system before it, contained within it the defects that would transform it—defects inherent in the institution of private property and the competitive system. The ruthless competition for profits would necessarily result in an increasing concentration of wealth in the hands of those who proved most able in the ruthless competition for profits, thereby reducing the laborers and the defeated capitalists to the level of a bare subsistance; and when this process reached a certain stage the system would collapse for the simple reason that there would be no profit in producing commodities when the underlying proletarian population was no longer able to purchase them at a price that would yield a profit. When this stage was reached, the proletariat, made class conscious by their misery, instructed in the dialectic of social change by their leaders, and united for the defense of their class interests, would by revolutionary action abolish private property in land and capital, and through a democratic government based upon a classless society, organize the production and distribution of wealth for the common good.

The Marxian doctrine provided a new and persuasive ideology for the oppressed working classes whose hopes were persistently defeated by liberal-democracy as a going concern. Its analysis of the capitalist system justified their grievances against their employers, while its philosophy of history promised them that all would be made right in the future, and assured them that in defending their class interests they could not fail since they were supported by the indefeasible forces that shaped the destiny of mankind.

Inspired by the Marxian faith, the industrial workers formed new political parties, for the most part called Socialist, and for the most part accepting the Marxian doctrine of the social revolution. But meantime, while waiting for the coming revolution, and as a preparation for it, the Socialist parties adopted a program of social legislation designed to benefit the masses at the expense of the classes. Attracted by this practical program, lower middle-class people, mostly timid folk who abhorred the idea of violence, voted in increasing numbers for Socialist candidates in the hope of benefiting from the legislation which the Socialist parties promised to support. One result of this trend in practical politics was that the Socialist parties derived their chief support from voters who were not Marxian socialists; another was that the leaders of the Socialist parties, in order to win and hold non-Marxian voters, found it necessary to soft-pedal the doctrine of imminent, catastrophic revolution. In the decade before the Great War the dominant Socialist parties had therefore virtually abandoned the Marxian conception of the revolution as a violent upheaval, and conceived of it as a slow and peaceful process in which the masses, by established political methods, would gain control of the government, and by normal legislative procedure within the existing democratic regime would abolish private property in land and capital and socialize the production and distribution of wealth.

During the Great War the influence of Socialism naturally declined, but the orthodox Marxian tradition, barely kept alive by minority groups within and without the dominant Socialist parties, was given a dramatic and world-wide significance by the Russian Revolution. As reinterpreted by Lenin and realized in the Soviet regime, neo-Marxianism took the name of Communism, and must be clearly distinguished from Socialism as understood by such prewar Socialists as Bernheim and Kautsky, and such present-day Socialists as Norman Thomas. Present-day Socialism and neo-Marxian Communism agree in one thing only— the necessity of abolishing private property in the means of production. In respect to the means for accomplishing this desired end they disagree radically. Socialism maintains that it can be accomplished by peaceful political methods within the framework of the existing democratic regime; Communism maintains that it can be accomplished only by violent revolutionary expropriation of the capitalist class, carried through for the masses by the dictatorship of a disciplined Communist party.

It was also an essential part of Communist theory that the establishment of Communism in one country would be the prelude to an international Communist revolution. So far, the prediction has not been realized. Revolutions there have been, in Italy, in Germany, in many European countries. But these revolutions, stimulated in part by the fear of Communism rather than by devotion to it, have taken the name of Fascist; and until recently at all events Communism and Fascism have been commonly regarded, especially by the Communists and Fascists themselves, as being fundamentally opposed to each other.

In respect to political theory there are certain differences between Communism and Fascism. In theory Communism maintains that the dictatorship, a drastic technique essential to the revolution but ending with it, will be replaced by a democratic government of free and equal individuals, while Fascism rejects the democratic ideal altogether in favor of the permanent dictatorship. In theory Communism professes to be international, while Fascism frankly accepts the doctrine of racial superiority and national egoism. In theory Communism recognizes the value of reason and science, while Fascism is essentially anti-intellectual in its subordination of reason to will.

In theory, yes; but the Soviet regime in Russia has failed, even more conspicuously than existing democratic societies, to harmonize theory and practice. Although the revolution has long since ended, the classless society has not emerged. The dictatorship is now more firmly established, the prospect for a democratic government is now more remote, than in the time of Lenin. The Stalin regime is no less nationalist and no more international than the regime of Hitler, and its regimentation of opinion and scholarship no less effectively subordinates reason to the will of the dictator. The revolution in Russia, as Trotsky said, has been betrayed; but it has been betrayed less by men and circumstances than by a radical contradiction in Communist theory. The rational and humane values proclaimed in Communist theory are frankly divorced from the means by which they can be realized; they are regarded as ideal ends projected into the future, but incapable of being attained except by the temporary resort to antirational and inhumane means. So far at least the result of this radical contradiction between ends and means has been, and as I think must under any circumstances have been, that the ideal ends were defeated by the very means employed to attain them.

It is in this fundamental discord between ends and means that Communism and Fascism, as they actually function, are alike—alike in the methods they employ and in the assumptions by which the methods are justified. The Communist and the Fascist revolutions were carried through by the same political technique and the same resort to naked force. The personal power of Mussolini and Hitler is no more arbitrary, more complete, or more ruthlessly employed than that of Stalin. Both

Communism and Fascism assume that the welfare of the community and the progress of mankind are in some mystical fashion identified with an abstract entity, called in the one case the dialectic of history and in the other the totalitarian state. Both assume that this abstract entity is realized in the person of an inspired leader to whom the truth has been revealed and the direction of affairs committed. Both assume that the individual, in comparison with the state or the dialectic process, has no significance except as an instrument to be used, with whatever degree of brutality may be necessary, for realizing ends which the leader judges to be good. Both do in effect, whatever they may proclaim in theory, subordinate reason to will, identify right with naked force as an instrument of will, and accord value to the disinterested search for truth only in so far as the leader judges it to be temporarily useful for the attainment of immediate political ends.

Communism and Fascism claim to be theoretical formulations of a "new order" in the world. But as revealed in their works they are no more than the recurrence of old political forms, that is to say, the recurrence in practice of what is variously known as tyranny, dictatorship, absolute monarchy; the recurrence in theory of what is known as divine right. As such they are alike, and alike at war with the fundamental values and assumptions which liberal-democracy, if it is to retain any significance, must preserve.

III

THE infinitely complicated process which we call history continuously gives rise to what are called social problems, and at the same time generates those political and intellectual trends which indicate the direction which the solution of those problems is likely to take. The term "solution," used in this connection, is misleading. It connotes a certain perfection or finality, comparable to the solution of a mathematical or a chemical problem, which is never possible in social relations. "The function of history," as J.B. Bury once remarked, "is not to solve problems but to transform them." In our time the historical process has given rise to the problem of the distribution of wealth, a problem which assumes the double form of social conflict within the nations and of diplomatic and military conflict between them. It would be naïve indeed to suppose that this problem, in either of its forms, will be "solved" with any notable degree of perfection or finality. It will be solved only in the sense of being transformed; and in looking for the direction which this transformation will take,

82

we must consult, not merely our hopes or our preferences, but also the dominant political and intellectual trends which the history of our time discloses.

Those political and intellectual trends I have discussed and discriminated under the terms Liberal-Democracy, Socialism, Communism, and Fascism. The differences between them, both as ideological systems and as going concerns, are obvious and important; but underneath their differences we can note, in respect to what they propose to do and are doing to solve the problem of the distribution of wealth, an interesting and significant similarity. It is a similarity of direction: all these systems are carrying us, with or without our consent, toward an extension of governmental regulation of economic enterprise.

That this is the direction is evident. In all liberal-democratic countries, for the last hundred years, there has been a steadily increasing amount of such regulation of economic enterprise. Both Communism and Socialism propose to make the regulation complete by abolishing private property in the means of production, and the Communist regime in Russia has already accomplished this object. Fascism, no less than Communism, proposes to subordinate the individual to the state; and in the principal Fascist countries,

83

although private property in land and capital has not been formally abolished, the national economy has been so far subjected to governmental direction that free economic enterprise has virtually disappeared. Like it or not, the complexities of a highly integrated technological civilization are carrying us in a certain direction, that is to say, away from freedom of the individual in economic enterprise and toward an extension of social control. This is therefore the direction which, in democratic as well as in other countries, the transformation of the problem of the distribution of wealth will surely take.

The question that chiefly concerns us is whether the necessary social regulation of economic enterprise can be effected by the democratic method, that is to say, without a corresponding social regimentation of opinion and political freedom. Can the possessors be sufficiently dispossessed and the dispossessed be sufficiently reinstated without resort to violence—to revolution and the temporary or the permanent dictatorship. The Communists say no—sooner or later the revolution. The Fascists say no—the totalitarian state is the only solution. They may of course be right. It is futile to suppose that democracy must survive because it accords with the law of nature or some transcendent increasing purpose. Nor can we dismiss the rise of dictatorship in half the world as a temporary aberration brought to birth by the ingenuity of sinister or psychopathic individuals. Common men, when sufficiently distressed, instinctively turn to the inspired leader; and dictatorship in our time, as in past times, is the normal price exacted for the failure of democracy to bind common men by their hopes and fears. The survival of democratic institutions thus depends, not upon the attractiveness or logical consistency of theories of government, but upon the possibility of effecting, by the pragmatic democratic method, a sufficient equalization of possessions and of opportunity to provide common men with what they will consent to regard as tolerable.

It may be said, it has often been said, that the most brilliant civilizations of the past have paid scant attention to the needs or desires of common men, that the oppression of common men was the price that had to be paid for those great and permanent achievements which we associate with the progress of mankind. It may be so, but it no longer matters. The very technology which gives peculiar form and pressure to the oppression of common men in our time has freed common men from the necessity of submitting to it. The time has gone by when common men could be persuaded to believe that destitution is in accord with God's will, or to rely upon the virtues of *noblesse oblige* to ease their necessities. Through education and the schools, through the press and the radio, common men are made aware of their rights, aware of the man-made frustration of their hopes, aware of their power to organize for the defense of their interests. Any civilization in our time, however brilliant or agreeable it may appear to its beneficiaries or to posterity, which fails to satisfy the desires of common men for decent living will be wrecked by the power of common men to destroy what seems to them no longer worth preserving. The ultimate task of democracy may be to establish a brilliant civilization; but its immediate task is the less exalted one of surviving in any form, and the condition of its survival is that it shall, even at the sacrifice of some of the freedoms and amenities of civilization as we have known it, provide for the essential material need of common men.

Considered as a problem in scientific engineering, providing for the material needs of common men presents no insuperable difficulties: the necessary resources, equipment, man power, and knowledge are available. Given Plato's ruling class of philosopher kings, and a docile population responding to suggestion as smoothly as molten iron yields to physical pressure, adequate wealth could be produced and equitably distributed. Unfortunately perhaps, there are no such philosopher kings; fortunately, there are no such docile people. Government is much less a matter of knowing what is good to be done than of persuading average human beings, stubbornly rooted in conventional habits of thought and action, to do what fallible intelligence judges on incomplete data to be for the moment necessary or desirable. Democratic government is a matter of persuading them to do it voluntarily by registering their wishes in the form of ballots freely given. In democratic countries, therefore, the measures taken for effecting a more equitable distribution of wealth can never be based solely upon the best scientific knowledge available; they can be such only as the majority of citizens will voluntarily sanction and the minority voluntarily submit to.

It is as essential that the minority should voluntarily submit to the measures taken as it is that the majority should voluntarily approve them. Democratic government rests upon the principle that it is better to count heads than it is to break them. The principle is a good one, but unfortunately men will not, under certain conditions, so regard it. By and large the principle works well enough so long as the issues to be decided do not involve those interests which men will always fight for rather than surrender. By and large, democratic government, being government by discussion and majority vote, works best when there is nothing of profound importance to discuss, when the rival party programs involve the superficial aspects rather than the fundamental structure of the social system, and when for that reason the minority can meet defeat at the polls in good temper since it need not regard the decision as either a fatal or a permanent surrender of its vital interests. When these happy conditions disappear democratic government is always in danger.

The danger has already proved fatal in many countries. It exists, although it may not prove fatal, even in those countries where the democratic tradition is most strongly intrenched. For in these countries too the insistent problem of the distribution of wealth is beginning to involve those fundamental class interests which do not readily lend themselves to friendly discussion and mutual concession. The flagrant inequality of possessions and of opportunity is creating an ever sharper differentiation between the beneficiaries of private property in the means of production and the masses whose present circumstances and future prospects depend less upon individual character and talent than upon the hazards of the business cycle. Accompanying this differentiation there has been and is going on a confused but persistent realignment of political parties: on the Right, conservative parties representing the beneficiaries of the system of free enterprise; on the Left, radical parties representing the poor and the dispossessed. As the divergence between Right and Left becomes sharper and more irreconcilable, moderate and conciliatory parties tend to disappear, and the rival party programs of the extreme groups, no longer confined to the superficial aspects of policy within the framework of the traditional system, are increasingly concerned with the validity of the assumptions on which the system rests. Underlying the question of the equitable distribution of wealth is the more fundamental question of the validity of the institution of private property as a means of effecting it. The present power of the possessing classes rests upon the institution of private property; the present distress of the masses is somehow involved in it. If the present discords should be prolonged and intensified, the danger is that the masses will turn to revolution rather than submit to a system which fails to relieve them, that the classes will welcome forcible repression rather than surrender a system which guarantees their power.

The danger is not one to be lightly dismissed. It is certainly greater than many profess to think. But for all that we need not be browbeaten, by dogmatic assumptions, into believing that the discords in the capitalist system cannot under any circumstances be corrected by the democratic procedure. It is an article of Communist faith, which many advanced liberals seem to accept as a matter of course, that history offers no instance of a ruling aristocracy which has surrendered its power voluntarily, and that accordingly nothing short of violent revolutionary expropriation will induce the capitalist class to surrender the power which the institution of private property now confers upon it.

The premise is correct enough, but the conclusion is a *non sequitur*. True enough, no ruling class has ever surrendered its power voluntarily, but it does not follow that no ruling class has ever surrendered its power except under compulsion of naked force. The Roman Patricians did not surrender their power voluntarily, on demand; but they nevertheless surrendered it, gradually, under pressure, without incurring the destruction of republican institutions. The English aristocracy did not surrender its power voluntarily; but since the eighteenth century it has, under pressure exerted through the democratic political procedure, conceded one strategic position after another. And indeed in all those countries where democratic institutions still persist, the capitalist classes have, during the last fifty years or more, conceded bit by bit much of the control over private property which they formerly possessed and once thought indispensable. There is no compelling reason to suppose that, in those countries where the democratic tradition is strongly intrenched, this process of increasing governmental regulation of economic enterprise should not continue, even to the point, if that should prove necessary, of a virtual if not a formal socialization of certain basic industries, without incurring the destruction of democratic institutions.

It is not a question of keeping what we have or scrapping it for some untried ideal social system. At best it is a question of sufficiently improving what we have to avoid the intolerable distress which if unrelieved ends in despair and the resort to violence. No infallible panacea for accomplishing this end is available. The desired end can be accomplished, if at all, only by the method of trial and error, by employing the best knowledge available, so far as it can be employed by the democratic political method, to effect those adjustments which will put idle money to work in productive enterprises and idle men to work at a living wage. What particular measures are best adapted to do this I am incompetent to say. It is for the experts to suggest the particular measures.

Since the experts disagree, the measures adopted, however carefully considered, will in the event no doubt be attended with unforeseen consequences calling for still further measures. That attempts to remedy the evil are not wholly successful is no reason for abandoning the task. Something must be done, and much must be attempted that a little may be gained. What is chiefly needed is time— time for experiment, for making mistakes and correcting them, time for the necessary adjustment in vested interests and the necessary psychological adaptation to new ideas, time for the slow crystallization of public opinion and for registering public opinion in legislative enactments by the cumbersome democratic technique.

It is true, of course, that there may not be time enough. There may not be time enough in any case. Technological advance has so accelerated the tempo and complicated the character of social change that present social ills can scarcely be properly diagnosed before they have been so far transformed that the proposed remedies are no longer adequate. But if time fails us, it will be less because of inherent defects in the capitalist system or the democratic procedure than because of the disastrous results of modern war in dislocating the national economy and in impairing the democratic morale.

IV

THE ultimate cause of war is to be found no doubt
in the nature of man. But the proximate cause is
to be found in the particular conditions of time
and place. Politically, the modern world is organized on the principle of the self-sufficiency and
the self-determination of the sovereign state; eco-
nomically, it is so far integrated that all countries
are more or less interdependent. The result is that
war in our time arises chiefly from the competitive
political struggle for economic advantage—for
land, markets, essential raw materials, and prefer-
ential opportunities for exploiting the undevel-
oped regions of the earth. A rational solution of
the conflict would involve either complete freedom of trade and competitive industrial enterprise throughout the world, or the international
allocation of commodities and industrial opportunities according to the legitimate needs of the
several countries. A rational solution is impossible,
however, because the rights of states are measured
by the power they can exert, and the decisions of
governments, and the attitudes of the people who
support governments, are so largely determined by
considerations of honor and prestige and deep-
seated national fears and animosities. It is true

that international conflicts may be, and often have been, mediated by friendly discussion and mutual concession. But such mediation is now more difficult than formerly. The profound divergence between the current ideologies makes friendly discussion between democratic countries on the one hand, and Communist and Fascist countries on the other, virtually impossible, and injects into their conflicts a fanatical and intransigent quality unknown since the religious wars of the sixteenth century. Thus in our time the perennial danger of war arising from economic conflict is at once increased and less easily obviated because of the fears and hatreds arising from the clash of discordant ideological systems.

War and the imminent danger of war may temporarily abate the social conflict in any country, but the ultimate effect can only be to diminish the possibility of resolving it by the democratic method. Political democracy is at best a slow and cumbersome method of managing the affairs of the community. In times of great emergency it is necessary to get things swiftly done, whether well done or not; and in the supreme emergency of war, when arms speak and laws are silent, the democratic liberties are inevitably subordinated to military efficiency. Nevertheless, the temporary eclipse of the democratic liberties is not what matters most. What chiefly matters is that war, by devoting the energies of the nation to destructive ends, disrupts the peacetime economy, impoverishes and demoralizes the people, and thereby intensifies the social conflict which tends to undermine the stability of democratic institutions.

In September, 1939, the imminent danger of war was replaced by war itself. The war is justified as a war for the defense of democracy and the restoration of social order in Europe. The last war was likewise justified: we were told, and at the time many of us confidently believed, that it was fought to make the world safe for democracy. We now know that an outstanding result of it was to make half of Europe safe for dictators. What the result of the present war may be no man can say; but it would be naïve indeed to suppose that it will do more than the last war did to strengthen democratic institutions throughout the world, or even in the countries where they still exist. On the contrary, if experience be any guide at all, we must suppose that the present war, like the last one, will intensify those economic and social conflicts which have already, in many countries, proved fatal to the democratic way of life.

This is not to say that war can or should always be avoided. If democratic institutions cannot be safeguarded by war, still less can they be safe-

95

guarded by submitting to aggressions designed to destroy them. It is not true that it takes two to make a quarrel. One can very easily make a quarrel if he gives a perverted mind to it; and a government as well as an individual can make a quarrel inevitable by deliberate and persistent aggression. In September, 1939, the choice presented to France and Great Britain was not between war or peace. They had to choose between making war at that time or sanctioning aggressions which there was every reason to think would be followed by still further aggressions, so that in the end the choice would be between submitting to conquest or fighting under less favorable conditions. In such a situation the relevant conclusion, it seems to me, is that although war, being the negation of the democratic idea, can in itself do nothing to safeguard democratic institutions, it may very well be the only means of safeguarding the independence of those countries where democratic institutions exist. The essential condition for preserving democratic institutions is the political independence of the people who wish to preserve them. In this sense, therefore, if in this sense only, war may be a means of defending democracy. For although the chances for the survival of democratic institutions in Europe will be less at the end of the present war than they would have been if there had been no war, the chances will still be better in a Europe in which France and Great Britain retain their independence than they could be in a Europe dominated by the present Nazi regime in Germany. It is possible that democratic institutions may disappear in England as a result of the war even if Great Britain wins the war; they are certain to disappear if Germany wins the war. If then democratic institutions are to be destroyed in any case, it seems on the whole better that they should be destroyed by their friends than by their enemies.

When we consider the problem of preserving democratic institutions broadly, from both the national and the international point of view, we seem to be helplessly caught in a vicious circle. We know that democratic institutions are threatened by social discords within the nations, and still more by war between them. We know that if we could avoid war it would be much easier to resolve our social discords, and that if we could resolve our social discords it would be much easier to avoid war. If we could do either of these things without the other, the future of democracy would be fairly secure; if we could do both of them it would be altogether so. Yet we know that social discords are a major cause of war, and that war is the one thing that will make it impossible, if anything does, to resolve our social discords. It is in such situations that reason succumbs to force, in such situations that dictators flourish and democracy declines.

It is possible that the crisis which confronts the modern world involves something more serious even than the collapse of democratic institutions. The contradictions in the capitalist system may be no more than symbols of a discord more profound —the discord between the physical power at our disposal and our capacity to make a good use of it. It is obvious at all events that the history of the last two centuries presents us with a disturbing paradox: whereas the application of reason to the mastery of the physical world has proceeded with unanticipated success and mounting optimism, the persistent effort to shape the world of human relations to humane and rational ends has been so far unavailing that we are oppressed with a sense of frustration and defeat.

Long ago it was said that man can more easily take a city than govern himself. Never was the saying more true than now. Never before has the intelligence of man placed so much material power at his disposal: never before has he employed the power at his disposal for the realization of purposes more diverse or more irreconcilable. The hand of man is subdued to what it works in, and the mind admires what the hand can accomplish.

Modern man is therefore enamored of mechanical force. Fascinated by the esthetic precision and sheer power of the instruments he has devised, he will use them for doing whatever by their aid can be done, in the confident expectation that what can be done with such clean efficiency must be worth doing. Thus the machines we have invented tend to enslave us. Compelling us to use them on their own terms, and to adjust our conduct to their virtues and limitations, they somehow generate social forces which, being too complex and too intangible to be easily understood, shape our lives to ends we do not will but cannot avoid.

In times past certain civilizations, long established, brilliant and prosperous and seemingly secure against mischance, slowly decayed and either disappeared altogether or were transformed past recognition and forgotten. What has happened many times in the history of mankind may happen again. There are no barbarian hosts without the gates, but there are plenty of potential barbarians within them. It is then within the range of possibility that the flagrant discord between the mechanical power at man's disposal and his capacity to make good use of it is carrying the world into another period of widespread and chronic confusion in which democracy will everywhere succumb to dictatorship, reason to naked force, and naked

force prove to be the prelude to another dark age
of barbarism.

I do not say that this will happen. I do not think
it will. But it is futile to suppose that it cannot
happen, futile to rely upon the saving grace of
some transcendent increasing purpose (a law of
nature, or dialectic of history, or totalitarian state)
to bring us in spite of ourselves to a predestined
good end. For the solution of our difficulties the
only available purposes are our own, the only available intelligence such as we can command. If then
democracy survives, if civilization in any tolerable
form survives, it will be because, in some favored
parts of the world the human mind remains un-
shackled and, aided by time and fortunate circumstances, proves capable of subordinating the
unprecedented material power at its command to
the achievement of rational and humane ends.
More obvious now even than in the seventeenth
century is the truth of Pascal's famous dictum:
"Thought makes the whole dignity of man; therefore endeavor to think well, that is the only morality." The chief virtue of democracy, and in the
long run the sole reason for cherishing it, is that
with all its defects it still provides the most favorable conditions for the maintenance of that dignity and the practice of that morality.